PAINTINGS OF
MAINE

Edited by Arnold Skolnick • Introduction by Carl Little

CLARKSON POTTER / PUBLISHERS
NEW YORK

A CHAMELEON BOOK

Copyright © 1991 by Chameleon Books, Inc.
Introduction © 1991 by Carl Little
Published by Clarkson N. Potter, Inc.
201 East 50th Street, New York, New York, 10022
Distributed by Crown Publishers, Inc.
Member of the Crown Publishing Group.
CLARKSON N. POTTER, POTTER and colophon
are trademarks of Clarkson N. Potter, Inc.

Produced by Chameleon Books, Inc.
211 West 20th Street
New York, N.Y. 10011

Production director / designer: Arnold Skolnick
Editiorial assistant: Nancy Crompton
Composition: Larry Lorber, Ultracomp, New York
Printed and Bound by O.G. Printing Productions, Ltd., Hong Kong

Library of Congress Cataloging-in-Publication Data

The Paintings of Maine / edited by Arnold Skolnick; introduction by
     Carl Little.
          p.   cm.
     ISBN 0-517-58229-5 : $27.50
     1. Landscape painting, American.   2. Maine in art.   3. Maine in
literature.   I. Skolnick, Arnold.   II. Little, Carl.
ND1351.P35   1991
758'.1741'0973 — dc20   90-22365
     ISBN: 0-517-58229-5   CIP
     10 9 8 7 6 5 4 3 2 1
     First Edition

(half-title page)
N. C. Wyeth, *Portrait of a Young Artist*, [Andrew Wyeth] c. 1930
Oil on canvas, 32 x 40 in.

(frontispiece)
George Wesley Bellows, *Romance of Autumn*, 1916
Oil on canvas, 32 ½ x 40 in.

(title page)
Leon Kroll, *Monhegan Landscape*, 1913
Oil on canvas, 8 ¾ x 10 ¾ in.

Acknowledgments

From Edna St. Vincent Millay, COLLECTED POEMS, New York,
Harper & Row, 1956. Copyright © 1954, 1982 by Norma Millay Ellis.
Reprinted by permission of Elizabeth Barnett, Literary Executor.

From RELATIONS, Selected Poems 1950–1985 by Philip Booth.
Copyright © 1986 by Philip Booth. Reprinted by permission of
Viking Penguin, a division of Penguin Books, USA Inc.

From WITH OPEN EYES by Marguerite Yourcenar. English transla-
tion: Copyright © 1984, by Beacon Press; French text copyright ©
1980 by Editions Du Centurion, Paris.

From Elizabeth Coatsworth, MAINE MEMORIES, 1968, reprinted
by permission of Kate Barnes.

Charles E. Wadsworth, THE COAST OF MAINE, reprinted by
permission of the author.

From Fairfield Porter, THE COLLECTED POEMS, edited by John
Yau with David Kermani. Copyright © Tibor de Nagy Editions, New
York, 1985.

From Georgia O'Keeffe, GEORGIA O'KEEFFE, 1976, Copyright ©
Juan Hamilton, 1987.

From Samuel French Morse, THE CHANGES, published by Alan
Swallow, Denver, 1964, reprinted by permission of Jane C. Morse.

Edward M. Holmes, A PART OF MAINE, University of Maine Press,
Orono Maine, 1973, reprinted by permission of the author.

From E. B. White, ESSAYS OF E. B. WHITE, 1979. Copyright ©
1955 by E. B. White. Reprinted by permission of Harper Collins
Publishers.

From Robert P. Tristram Coffin, MAINSTAYS OF MAINE, 1945,
reprinted by permission of Richard N. Coffin.

Chameleon Books is enormously grateful to all the public and private
collectors and art galleries who have supplied the wonderful images
found in this book. We are especially indebted to: Marguerite Lavin
from the Brooklyn Museum; Anita Duquette from the Whitney
Museum of American Art; and Mel Ellis from the New Britain Museum
of American Art.

     We also wish to express our gratitude to the Maine instituitions
and their curators, who have so warmly opened up their collections
of Maine paintings: Katherine Watson from the Bowdoin College
Museum of Art; Hugh J. Gourley III from the Colby College Museum
of Art; Michael Culver from the Museum of Art of Ogunquit;
Martha Severens of the Portland Museum of Art; and special thanks

to Suzette McAvoy from the William A. Farnsworth Library and Art Museum.

We are grateful to the following galleries for their assistance: Brooke Alexander; Grace Borgenicht; Hirschl & Adler Modern; Hobes Sound North; Marlborough; Taggart & Jorgensen; Tibor De Nagy; and Vose. Thanks to Roger Howlett from the Childs; Leigh Morse from Coe Kerr; William E. O'Reilly from Salander O'Reilly; Carol Pesner and Katherine Kaplan of the Kraushaar; and special thanks to Thomas Crotty from the Frost Gully Gallery.

Our thanks to the many contemporary artists and to the following private collectors: Barney Ebsworth, Arthur G. Altschul, and Myron Kunin from the Regis Collection.

We are very grateful to the staff of Clarkson N. Potter: Howard Klein, whose art direction has given the book its special look; Catherine Sustana, who kept everything going; and Lauren Shakely whose ear for language and eye for painting has been greatly appreciated.

Arnold Skolnick

I would like to second Arnold Skolnick's words of appreciation, with special thanks extended to Suzette McAvoy, Judith Sobol, Katherine Watson, Martha Severens, Hugh Gourley, Katherine Lattanzi and their respective museum staffs for their help and hospitality; and to Thomas Crotty, Rosemarie Frick, Jil Eaton, Bridget Moore, John Payson, Carol Pesner and the other gallery proprietors who have contributed to this book.

Also to be acknowledged are the art historians, scholars and critics whoe work has inspired my own: Lloyd Goodrich, James Carpenter, John I.H. Bauer, et al., authors of *Maine and Its Role in American Art, 1740–1963*; Christopher Huntington, who wrote the lucid text for the 1964 exhibition "Maine: 100 Artists of the 20th Century"; Alan Gussow, whose *A Sense of Place: The Artist and the American Land* (1972) remains a landmark art book; Bruce Robertson, organizer of the show "Reckoning with Winslow Homer: His Late Paintings and Their Influence," currently touring the states; and Edgar Allen Beem, *Maine Times* critic and author of the excellent *Maine Art Now* (1990).

Of particular importance to my overall growth as a critic was John Wilmerding's "Introduction to Art" course, which I attended as an undergraduate at Dartmouth College. Wilmerding's contribution to our understanding of American art continues to be invaluable.

Paintings of Maine is dedicated to my parents and siblings; to Peggy, Emily and James, my Somesville loved ones; and to Uncle Buster, aka William Kienbusch, who put me on to Maine painting many years ago, and whose own art sustains me still.

Carl Little

Contents

INTRODUCTION
6

ARTISTS' BIOGRAPHIES
120

SELECTED MAINE MUSEUMS
121

CREDITS
124

WHEN I ARRIVE IN MAINE, I START SEEING AGAIN," THE PAINTER WILLIAM KIENBUSCH ONCE SAID, AN ASSERTION THAT SUCCINCTLY EXPRESSES THE ALLURE OF THIS VAST NORTHEASTERN STATE TO SO MANY ARTISTS. MAINE, KIENBUSCH'S WORDS IMPLY, CONFERS ON THOSE WHO PAINT ITS LANDSCAPES A

clear-eyed breadth of view not available anywhere else. Add a stunning and multifarious topography to this clarity of vision, and you've got a *plein air* painter's paradise.

Acknowledging its geographical expanse, novelist Mary McCarthy once described Maine as being "less a state than a country." Several thousand miles of seacoast, islands by the score; mighty rivers, a multitude of gemlike lakes; farms and woodland stretching wide under tall skies, accented with impressive peaks—with this panoramic bounty, it comes as no surprise that Maine has attracted a lion's share of landscape painters; more, perhaps, than any other state in the Union. From Thomas Cole's generation in the early 1800s, through Homer, Marin, Hartley and Hopper, up to Porter, Wyeth and Welliver, and younger generations today, the destination has been this northernmost New England state, whose spell, though chipped away at by civilization and its

discontents, continues to be cast far and wide.

Even many a Maine-born artist has made this journey, called back from the cities of the world by the prospect of pristine skies, phantom fogs, savage gales. The best-known example of this "return of the native" is Marsden Hartley (1877–1943). Born in Lewiston, Maine's second-largest city, located on the Androscoggin River, Hartley left home early on to see the world, but only truly discovered himself as a painter when he returned in the late 1930s. Having by then tried on all manner of stylistic hats, he was finally and fully prepared to reclaim Maine with brush and canvas.

Hartley's views of Mount Katahdin in northern Maine (the second-highest mountain in New England) rival Cézanne's of Mont St.-Victoire, while his seascapes further the dynamic vision of Cole, Homer and other devotees of nature in its more primal guises. Although he did not

ELIZABETH B. ROBINSON, View of North Monmouth, Maine, c. 1862, Pastel on paper, 15½ x 21½ inches

GINA WERFEL. Rocks at High Tide, 1988, Oil on linen, 28 x 36 inches

receive the hero's homecoming he had hoped for (most eyes were turned to the latest dispatches from Europe), Hartley nevertheless embraced his native state, in painting as well as in poems and essays. In his oft-quoted discourse, "On the Subject of Nativeness — A Tribute to Maine" (1937), Hartley voices the kind of Romantic ideal which has been, and remains, the credo of so many Maine painters — that come hell or high water or World War, the land's essential qualities will endure: "If the Zeppelin rides the sky at night, and aeroplanes set flocks of sea gulls flying, the gulls remain the same and the rocks, pines, and thrashing seas never lose their power and their native tang."

Distinguishing between those individuals born and bred in Maine and those who have come "from away" is a favorite sport of the critics in this state, nativeness being an honor hardwon, if winnable at all ("please show your genealogies at the door," the sign might read for newcomers). The painters featured in this book are primarily out-of-staters, yet the majority of them have made a sustained commitment to their adopted state through their art.

Take Winslow Homer (1836–1910): though born in Boston, Homer could trace a good part of his family roots to Maine, and his removal to Prout's Neck (about ten miles south of Portland) in 1884 sealed his marriage to what the writer Sarah Orne Jewett called "the country of the pointed firs." Homer's devotion to this rocky point of land was all-encompassing, and he built his studio where he could best experience the elements. "The life I have chosen gives me full hours of enjoyment for the balance of my life," he once stated: "The sun will not rise, or set, without my notice, and thanks." His was an exacting eye — "I can tell in a second if an outdoors picture with figures has been painted in a studio," he once boasted — and he was no-nonsense with his advice to fellow landscape painters: "Never put more than two waves in a picture," he counseled Leon Kroll (1884–1974). "It's too fussy."

With this last comment in mind, one wonders what Homer would have made of the lively, wave-filled coastal views of John Marin (1870–1953). Like Homer, Marin was born outside Maine, in Rutherford, New Jersey; yet as an artist he spent so many seasons exploring the craggy coastline that in his letters to Alfred Stieglitz, his New York dealer, he could complain, like a true native, about the intrusion of summer people. His oils and watercolors provide overwhelming proof of his allegiance to Maine. Indeed, Marin's "riptide paint," in poet Philip Booth's formulation, is "more Maine / than Maine."

A passage from one letter of Marin's, sent to Stieglitz from Cape Split in 1940, underscores the interrelatedness of the artists in Maine, and how one generation connects with another in spite of the great breadth of the state:

> Three weeks ago a young man arrived — he's something of a boy — stayed overnight — *insisted on helping* — met him at Rosenfeld's — paints — showed me some drawings — good — his name Porter — brother of man you gave photographic exhibition to — I guess they're two mighty fine fellows.

This "something of a boy" was Fairfield Porter (1907–1975), brother of the well-known nature photographer Eliot Porter; he had sought out the "Ancient Marin-er," as Marin once referred to himself, in his secluded downeast outpost to pay his respects to the master. Porter would go on to become a formidable creator of Maine seascapes in his own right, summering on Great Spruce Head Island in Penobscot Bay, where he found the requisite isolation, and natural beauty, to sustain his art.

Another painter who made a pilgrimage to Cape Split was William Kienbusch (1914–1980). Kienbusch, like Porter, was a fervent admirer of the elder statesman of Maine coast art. In an interview published in the *Ellsworth American* in 1967, Kienbusch displayed the straightforward honesty of his mentor, Marin, as in the following serious-humorous remarks:

> What I don't like about the Maine landscape is the postcard aspect you see in what is for sale, in pictures in magazines. I can't stand the goddamned lobster buoys and

WILLIAM KIENBUSCH, Across Penobscot Bay, 1955, Gouache on paper, 27 x 40½ inches

Rockwell Kent. Toilers of the Sea, 1907, Oil on canvas, 38 x 44 inches

driftwood and lighthouses and all that saccharin. That stuff is what drove a friend of mine to stand up in his boat and announce that he would like to kick a Maine sea gull in the behind.

SIMILAR generational linkages, as well as simple word of mouth, have played a critical role in the migration of artists to Maine. Ogunquit, Monhegan Island, and Mount Desert Island are three Maine locales whose artistic heritages have to a great extent been shaped by this passing along of the esthetic baton.

The first of these, located on the coast between Portsmouth, New Hampshire, and Portland, Maine, is perhaps the only place in the state that can truly claim to be an art colony. Ogunquit's evolution as a gathering place for painters and sculptors began in the late 1800s, with the arrival of Charles H. Woodbury (1864–1940), a young art teacher from Boston. As is recounted in *A Century of Color, 1886–1986*, a fascinating history of the colony, Woodbury's enthusiastic response to the area set off a kind of chain reaction: "...it was not long before artists' easels dotted the rocks and ridges of Perkins Cove, the beach, the roadsides and the fields and meadows of Ogunquit."

Maurice Prendergast, Edward Hopper, Leon Kroll, Yasuo Kuniyoshi, Walt Kuhn, Waldo Pierce, Antonio Mattei, and Beverly Hallam are but a handful of the distinguished artists who have worked in this relatively small section of Maine coast. Mattei (1900–1956) was an early member of the Ogunquit Art Association, founded in 1928; his treatment of certain coastal subjects reveals a sense of mystery and fancy. Likewise, Japanese-born Kuniyoshi (1893–1953)

responded to the landscape in an out-of-the-ordinary manner which approached surrealism. Many art historians feel Kuniyoshi did some of his finest work in the half-dozen or so summers he spent in the area.

For a number of artists, Ogunquit has been simply a picturesque spot in which to practice one's art a few months each summer. One painter who staked a year-round claim was Niles Spencer (1893–1952), who first arrived to study with Woodbury in the summers of 1914–15. The three years (1919–22) he and his wife lived in Ogunquit proved highly significant to Spencer's growth as a Precisionist painter. He later recalled the lasting impression this period left on him, and, in so doing, offered an alternative view of the legendary mean Maine winters:

> The winters came as a revelation. I had more or less expected bleakness, cold and lonely isolation, but the actuality was quite different. The storms, the clear cold sunlight and especially the quiet silvery gray days when the sea, sky and land achieved a total relationship, made the bright blue, the lush green of summer, seem crude and far away...The contact with the winter scene at this time, when the underlying structure of the whole landscape stood out so clearly, affected the whole direction of my future work. It left me with the obvious but basic conviction that wherever art ends it begins with nature.

"ART...begins with nature": so might be the embarkation cry of the numerous artists who have made the boat trip out to Monhegan Island (ten miles from Port Clyde, twenty from Boothbay Harbor), lured by reports of its spectacular headlands, its stark, ironbound beauty. If, as William Cullen Bryant once remarked, "Art sighs to carry its conquests into new realms," this 600-odd acres worth of ledge and meadow, moor and spruce and balsam fir forest set out in the Atlantic has had a superabundance of sighers.

The most famous of Monhegan's art lineages runs from Robert Henri (1865–1929), a leading member of New York's Ashcan School, to his students Rockwell Kent (1882–1971), George Wesley Bellows (1882–1925) and Edward Hopper (1882–1967). Henri himself had found his way to the island through the instigation of fellow painter Edward Willis Redfield (1869–1965), who practiced a kind of academic impressionism during the thirty or so years he worked in Maine.

Kent showed up on the island in 1905, Bellows in 1911, and Hopper in 1916, all three invited by Henri, who, according to art historian Lloyd Goodrich, had first begun to work there as early as 1903. This trio of formidable New York-based artists would hungrily paint up this island world, entranced, after the sooty existence of the city, by the translucent air, dramatic cliffs, sturdy fisherfolk and their simple shacks, and, above all else, by the rocks and awe-inspiring sea.

"Probably for no better reason than that I was born in Westchester County, which has practically no seacoast," wrote Kent in an essay in 1928, "I wanted more than anything to live on the ocean; so I went to Monhegan Island." That he was impressed by what he found is evidenced in his autobiography, *It's Me O Lord* (1955), where he writes:

> It [Monhegan] was enough for me, enough for all my fellow artists, for all of us who sought "material for art." It was enough to start me off to such feverish activity in

painting as I had never known.

Quite a claim for an island only one and one-half miles long by three-quarters of a mile wide, and yet Kent's extraordinary landscapes and those of so many other artists who've worked on Monhegan bear him out a thousand times over—as does the fact that today the island's summer artists' group boasts around twenty-five members.

Bellow's response to Monhegan equaled Kent's for sheer ecstasy: "This is the most wonderful country ever modeled by the hand of the master architect," he wrote to his wife Emma in 1911. Bellows brought to bear on the island landscape his own particular brand of realism, which owed much of its power to his deployment of energetic, near-sculptural brushstrokes, an approach encouraged by Henri.

The equally commanding oil sketches Edward Hopper made on Monhegan in the summers of 1916–19 were, to his mind, unfinished works, and he consequently refused to show them. Yet, as the art historian Bruce Robertson recently pointed out, "Hopper rarely attained such forceful expression of the momentary flux and chaos of nature as on Monhegan." He also did brilliant work later on in Ogunquit and on Cape Elizabeth.

RETURNING to the mainland, and to Rockwell Kent, we note another teacher-student rapport, that of Kent and Stephen Etnier (1903–1984). Born in York, Pennsylvania, Etnier attended the Yale Art School and the Pennsylvania Academy of the Fine Arts, both briefly, before studying with Kent. In 1928, he talked the master into taking him on as an apprentice; two years later, he began his long affair with the coast of Maine.

STEPHEN MORGAN ETNIER, Mid-Channel Bell, 1954, Oil on canvas, 11 x 24 inches

Piers, marinas, wharves, docks and other staples of the coastal scene were among Etnier's favorite motifs; he found them in Phippsburg, South Freeport, Harpswell, Portland and many more locations in the state. What is perhaps most remarkable about his landscapes is their utter calm. Largely eschewing the better-known, near-cliché crashing sea pictures, Etnier opted for the mirror-flat cove, the windless bay. In so doing, he looked back not to Homer, but to Fitz Hugh Lane (1804–1865), one of the most important of the Luminist painters, who also favored still waters.

Lane was one of a dozen or so artists who worked on Mount Desert Island around the middle of the nineteenth century, incited to make the long voyage downeast by tales of unprecedented natural beauties — ones that might even rival those of the Hudson River. While John Greenleaf Whittier painted a rather severe picture of the island — now the site of Acadia National Park — in his poem-legend "Mogg Megone" —

> The gray and thunder-smitten pile
> Which marks afar the Desert Isle

— others better acquainted with this stretch of the Maine coast came up with descriptions that must have made the landscape painters of the day champ at the bit.

A good example of such an enticing portrayal is found

in Clara Barnes Martin's guide, *Mount Desert, On the Coast of Maine,* an exquisitely written account of the area first published in 1867, and reprinted as many as eight times before the end of the century. Martin writes:

> The exact expression of the special character of Mount Desert, which, as it were, culminates the wonder of the [Maine] coast, involves antitheses and contrasts often employed in the creation of poetic fancy, but here, absolutely necessary to convey any adequate idea of the country. Bleak mountain-side and sunny nook in sheltered cove — frowning precipice and gentle, smiling meadow — broad, heaving ocean and placid mountain lake — dashing sea-foam and glistening trout-brook — the deep thunder of the ground-swell and the solemn stillness of the mountain gorge — the impetuous rush and splash of the surf and the musical cadence of far-off water-falls — all mingle and blend in the memory of this wonderful land.

Though not the first artist to arrive on this spectacular scene, British-born Thomas Cole (1801–1848) is, like Charles Woodbury in Ogunquit, generally credited with having opened up the Mount Desert Island area to fellow seekers of the natural sublime. Cole was a true champion of landscape painting; in his famous "Essay on American Scenery" (1836), he sounded the trumpet for the great outdoors, calling it "...the exhaustless mine from which the poet and the painter have brought such wondrous treasures."

In an article published in 1850, Joseph L. Stevens, Jr. described in great detail a trip he made to the Mount Desert Island area with fellow Gloucesterman Fitz Hugh Lane. Like Cole, Stevens was instrumental in calling the public's, and many an artist's, attention to this particular portion of Maine's splendors. Note how his enthusiasm for the area matches Cole's:

> The beauties of this place is [sic] well known and appreciated among artists. Lane who was with us, made good additions to his portfolio. But how unsatisfying a few days to an artist, when many months sketching would scarcely suffice amid such exhaustless wealth of scenery.

Lane had indeed made "good additions to his portfolio": his views of Somes Sound, the fiord that cuts into the center of Mount Desert, are among his greatest achievements as a painter, displaying a sense of light that is, quite simply, magical. As John Wilmerding notes in his excellent monograph on Lane, the artist's "Maine view almost eliminates the human presence and makes light (with all its symbolism) the dominant element of his landscape."

Another painter who seems to have been blessed with a built-in light meter was Frederic E. Church (1826–1900), Cole's sole pupil. Church, too, made a point of voyaging to Mount Desert Island, where he discovered sunsets perfectly suited to his Romantic sensibility. Like Kent, who also spent time in Alaska, Newfoundland and Tierra del Fuego, "among other out-of-the-way places," Church was forever setting forth for the ends of the earth in search of suitable "material for art." It is no wonder, then, that he also found his way to Mount Katahdin, approximately 120 miles north of Mount Desert, not far from Maine's border with Canada.

The oil sketches Church produced on his several sojourns to inland Maine seem far removed from the exacting grandeur for which he is so well known. Confronted with what was then largely uncharted wilderness — what Thoreau, in *The Maine Woods* (1834), called "that Earth of which we have heard, made out of Chaos and Old

Night"—perhaps Church felt more comfortable in an unrestrained, near-abstract mode, although he did execute some stunning representational views of Katahdin rising grandly out of the sea of virgin timber.

IT IS quite natural that a state with so much dramatic coastline to offer has inspired a great many marine painters to their finest work. Overlapping generations of artists from the eighteenth to the twentieth centuries have plied the Maine seaboard with their easels, sketchpads, brushes and paint, stopping to do a view of Camden harbor, the Mount Desert Rock lighthouse, Cape Elizabeth, Penobscot and Frenchman's Bay or an island or two. Painters like Thomas Doughty (1793–1856), Alvan Fisher (1792–1863), Charles Codman (1800–1842), John Bradley Hudson, Jr. (1832–1903) and William Partridge Burpee (1846–1940) excelled at the marinescape—the Mainescape—relishing the leap of wave, the thrust of headland, the peace of ships at anchor.

By contrast, in the history of Maine art, painters of the

WILLIAM PARTRIDGE BURPEE, Misty Morning, Blackhead, c. 1920, Oil on canvas, 6¾ x 12⅛ inches

state's interior are few and far between, although even as these words are written more and more landscape artists are turning away from the picture-postcard coast toward the less-heralded woodlands. Two of the youngest of the contemporaries featured in this book—Alan Bray (b. 1946) and Rush Brown (b. 1948)—have trained their eyes and palettes on a Maine unknown to many a visitor to "Vacationland," the state's license plate designation.

One painter who consecrated much of his artistic energy to Maine's inland beauty was Carl Sprinchorn (1887–1971). Born in Broby, Sweden (he was truly "from away"), Sprinchorn moved in 1903 to New York City where he promptly enrolled in Robert Henri's class at William Merritt Chase's New York School of Art. Knowing no English, but willing to work and to learn, the young Swede soon won the attention of his professor, who made him manager of the Robert Henri School of Art in 1907.

That same year, Sprinchorn made his first trip to Maine, followed by another four years later, but it wasn't until 1917 that he began to set aside periods of time to explore and paint the Maine woods. Unlike many a contemporary who would set up his or her studio on some pleasant stretch of coast, Sprinchorn stayed in lumber camps, shunning the summer social scene for Maine at its chilliest and most isolated.

In a letter to Ettie Stettheimer, written from the Swedish colony of Monson, Maine, in December 1920, Sprinchorn rhapsodizes about the severe beauty that had followed an ice storm:

> I wish you could have seen...it rained icy stuff all night, everything was like glass in the morning—the trees loaded to the breaking point, and they did break—all day it sounded as if tigers and elephants were crashing through the woods, snapping crackling as if guns...and the weirdly beautiful removed look of it all—! A little glass world shut in by a gray smoke coloured mist.

A fellow artist who admired Sprinchorn's work was Marsden Hartley. Following a chance encounter in New York in 1916, they went on to establish a long and voluminous correspondence. Judith H. O'Toole, writing of Sprinchorn's "realist impulse and Romantic vision," provides an amusing account of the kinship between these two loner painters:

> Hartley's interest in the coast and Sprinchorn's interest in the interior caused them to jokingly claim "hands off" to each other's territories and dub each other "King of the Coast" and "King of the Woods," respectively.

In more recent times, Neil Welliver (b. 1929) has gone to the Maine woods for his central subject matter, exhibiting the same "vividness and veracity" Hartley found in Sprinchorn's work. A year-round resident of Lincolnville, in the midcoast region, Welliver first came to the area to visit fellow painter Alex Katz (b. 1927). "I realized I was in the right place when I hit China Lakes and Palermo," he recounted to Edgar Allen Beem, the *Maine Times* art critic. "The people seemed sane to me. Like they hadn't lost their marbles yet."

Welliver's large landscapes range between tree- and rock-filled "interiors" to more open vistas of inland lakes, streams and beaver ponds; he has also tackled the lovely blueberry barrens. "Here there is incredible clarity," the painter says of Maine, reiterating the primacy of seeing that William

NEIL WELLIVER, Drowned Cedars, 1977, Oil on canvas, 96 x 120 inches

CHILDE HASSAM, *August Afternoon—Appledore*, 1900
Oil on canvas, 22¼ x 18 inches

Kienbusch and so many other artists have remarked upon. While the work of a human hand and state-of-the-art pigments, the intensely blue skies and waters in many of Welliver's paintings are not far from the truth, nor is the nearly laundered look of the light. In his poem "Light From Canada" (1972), James Schuyler describes this unadulterated light as

> scoured and Nova
> Scotian and of a clarity that
> opens up the huddled masses
> of the solid spruce so you
> see them in their bustling
> individuality.

Welliver thrives on his environment to the extent that, like a number of his fellow landscape artists in the state, he has become an "eco-freak," working to rescue the land from the grasp of despoiling landmongers and coal-burning plant enthusiasts. It's a concern that did not confront earlier painters in Maine, although references to preservation may be found as far back as Thomas Cole's "Essay on American Scenery" (1836), in which he remarks, "...it would be well to cultivate the oasis that yet remains to us, and thus preserve the germs of a future and purer system.

OFTEN pictured as a culturally insular state, Maine has nevertheless been indelibly marked by the world beyond its borders—which, of course, has included the world of art. On a number of occasions, particularly around the turn of the century and on into the esthetically charged 1910s and 20s, artists have borne the various "isms" of the day into this northern clime, reinventing the landscape before

these schools were Impressionism, Expressionism and Cubism, all of which were practiced in Maine, with some very impressive results.

Exemplary of the first school was the work of Childe Hassam (1859–1935), who brought his bright palette to bear on the stark yet beautiful shoreline of the Isles of Shoals, a group of small islands located nine miles out to sea from Portsmouth, New Hampshire, and sixteen from Cape Neddick, Maine. The boundary line between these two states cuts through the isles; Hassam worked primarily on Appledore, the largest of them, which falls within Maine's jurisdiction.

Hassam first traveled to the Isles of Shoals in the early 1880s, following the lead of Celia Thaxter, a Bostonian whose family had developed Appledore into a summer resort with a decidedly literary and artistic bent. In her informal history of the area, *Among the Isles of Shoals* (1873), Thaxter waxes poetic as regards the particular appeal of the place to the "urban refugees" of her day:

> The eternal sound of the sea on every side has a tendency to wear away the edge of human thought and perception; sharp outlines become blurred and softened like a sketch in charcoal; nothing appeals to the mind with the same distinctness as on the mainland, amid the rush and stir of people and things.

Frank W. Benson (1862–1951) worked in a related impressionist style on North Haven Island, off the coast from Rockland, Maine, starting in 1901, drinking in the same summer glories Hassam captured in his canvases. This school also took hold in Ogunquit, where Mabel May Woodward (1877–1945), among others, recorded various

MARSDEN HARTLEY, Birds of the Bagaduce, 1939
Oil on canvas, 28 x 22 inches

REUBEN TAM, Ocean Morning, 1957, Oil on canvas, 36 x 45 inches

seaside scenes with great panache. She may have crossed paths with Maurice Prendergast (1861–1924), who was equally taken with the colony's summer side of life.

Expressionism has been another major force in the development of Maine landscape painting, particularly as pursued in its more abstract mode by the likes of William Kienbusch and Reuben Tam (b. 1916). As an aspiring artist living on the island of Kauai, Hawaii, Tam had reproductions of some of Rockwell Kent's Monhegan pictures hanging in his room. In the survey *Art USA Now* (1963), Helen Hiller relates the unusual circumstances which led to Tam's discovering another well-known Maine painter:

> At the age of 24, he went to California for a vacation, carrying with him some paintings and poems. Exploring the cliffs along San Francisco, he saw a snake and followed it. It led him to a big building near the water—the Palace of the Legion of Honor. Inside was an exhibition of paintings by Marsden Hartley, paintings of the sea. Tam went to see the director, Thomas C. Howe, and was invited to bring his paintings. Four months later he had his first one-man show there.

Via New York, Long Island and Cape Cod, Tam eventually made his way to Monhegan Island, his summer home from 1948 to 1980. Influenced by the Abstract-Expressionist paintings he was seeing in New York, Tam employed a modified, nature-based version of this then-burgeoning esthetic to treat the rugged edges and brilliant tidal pools of Monhegan. He experimented with light and horizon, and rediscovered his love of geological subjects.

Tam's first summer on Monhegan coincided with Milton Avery's only season spent in Maine, on nearby Pemaquid Point. Though short-lived, Avery's stay resulted in a number of superb pictures which display his signature Fauve-like color schemes and his mastery of simplified forms.

Another kind of expressionism marks the Maine landscapes of Karl Schrag (b. 1912), who like Sprinchorn, emigrated to New York City as a young man, in his case from Karlsruhe, Germany. Schrag's relationship with Maine has been a long and fruitful one, with summers spent on Spruce Head Island, Friendship, Vinalhaven, and finally Deer Isle, his home away from home (which is Manhattan) for many years now. Nurtured on Expressionism, and a master etcher, Schrag frequently combines bold calligraphic strokes with vivid colors in his Maine coast subjects. One of his specialties has been the nocturne; indeed, he is one of the few Maine artists to treat this subject with consistent success.

The influences of cubism and other modernist tendencies were also felt in Maine, as revealed in the canvases of, among others, Marguerite (1887–1968) and William Zorach (1887–1966). It was art historian John I. H. Bauer, in his essay in *Maine and Its Role in American Art,* who made the telling observation that many of the artists, the Zorachs included, who attempted to handle the Maine landscape with the diverse tools of modernism, ended up working in a more traditional manner after a few years in the state—tamed, as it were, by the head-on power of the environment. Marguerite Zorach's Cubist period in Maine, for example, did not last long, although while it did, she brought a fresh perspective to some of the coast's time-honored motifs such as harbor views and townscapes, especially in and around Stonington in the early 1920s.

Like several other Maine-related artists of this century,

the Zorachs handed their artistic know-how on to one of their children. The work of Dahlov Ipcar (b. 1917), who has lived and made art at Robinhood Farm on Georgetown Island since 1937, bears little resemblance to that of her parents, although the animal pictures and children's book illustrations for which she is renowned at times disclose certain modernist traits. Ipcar has also tackled landscape subjects: *Rangeley October* (1984) celebrates the wildlife and fall foliage which can be found by this magnificent lake in western Maine.

WITHOUT a doubt the "first family" of Maine landscape painting is the Wyeths, whose artistic lineage stretches a full three generations—over 100 years of creating art, with no sign of diminishment—beginning with N. C. (1882–1945), then Andrew (b. 1917) and finally Jamie Wyeth (b. 1946). All three represent the vital vein of realism in Maine painting, one which forcefully reproduces nature and figures as they exist in real life, with a large dash of poetic romanticism added to help carry them into the realm of the larger-than-life.

N. C. Wyeth, who lived most of his life in Chadds Ford, Pennsylvania, began summering at Port Clyde (then called Herring Gut) in 1920, having been introduced to the area ten years earlier by fellow painter Sydney Chase. There Wyeth escaped the arduous existence of a much sought-after illustrator to paint in oils. His portraits of fishermen and his views of nearby Cannibal Shore (so-called for all the vessels and sailors it had swallowed alive) bring to mind Winslow Homer's Prout's Neck pictures; in fact, Wyeth even called his Port Clyde home "Eight Bells" after the latter's famous picture.

While N. C. Wyeth's figures are for the most part anonymous, those of his son Andrew are anything but: the life-worn visage of Christina Olson has been stamped on the eyes of America; it seems we know her face as well as we know that of a member of our own family. The placement of Christina and other Maine folk in an oftentimes somber Maine site—a brown field, a rudimentary kitchen or bedroom—adds another dimension to the sometimes brutal humanness of Wyeth's portraits.

Andrew Wyeth once likened arriving in Maine to "going on the surface of the moon," an impression supported by many of his views of the pared-down landscape around his home in Cushing. Technically brilliant, sober and poetically tough, Wyeth's vision of Maine recalls the words of Lew Dietz, one of the state's foremost cultural commentators, found in his classic *Night Train at Wiscasset Station* (1977):

> Maine was and still is a frontier. Maine people continue to be engaged in a battle with nature and an austere environment.

Jamie Wyeth has been summering on Monhegan Island since the 1960s, having first sailed to the island when he was fifteen. He bought the house Rockwell Kent had built for his mother overlooking Lobster Cove, the subject of Wyeth's painting *Kent House* (1972). Like Kent, Wyeth has discovered seemingly limitless "material for art" on Monhegan; as he stated to Martin Dibner, a Maine critic and writer, back in the early 1970s, "I could stay right on this point and spend the rest of my life painting."

When Kent returned to Monhegan in the late 1940s he

ANDREW WYETH, Night Hauling, 1944, Tempera on canvas, 23 x 37¼ inches

was disturbed to find his island transformed into what he called "a Down East Provincetown." Jamie Wyeth, too, is chagrined by the changes that have been taking place on his island refuge. Indeed, he is one of only a handful of contemporary Maine painters who've directly addressed the problem of rampant tourism in their art. A piece like *Excursion Boats* (1982) is downright editorial in its message: a woman dressed in old-fashioned clothing, seated in an antique wicker cart, gazes out at four boatloads of sightseers cutting across her view.

Another Monhegan resident, and painter, the late actor Zero Mostel was equally irked by seafaring intruders, but his response was more tongue-in-cheek and verbal, not visual: according to Martin Dibner, in his fine book *Sea-*

JAMIE WYETH, Excursion Boats, 1982, Mixed media on paper, 25¼ x 36⅛ inches

coast Maine (1973), Mostel "was known to stand on the crowded boat landing as the *Laura B.* came alongside with yet another boatload of tourists, waving it off and shouting, 'Plague! Plague! Cholera! Go back!'"

JAMIE WYETH is but one of a growing number of top-notch landscape painters working in Maine today. To verify this fact, one need only consult the recently published *Maine Art Now*, a compilation of *Maine Times* critic Edgar Allen Beem's reviews of the art scene from the past ten years or so. Landscapes abound in the pages of this book, ranging from those of past masters like Kienbusch, Porter and Etnier, to the latest work of Eric Hopkins (b. 1951), who has taken to the air in order to capture Maine from a wholly different viewpoint.

Living the year round on North Haven, Hopkins has excelled in rendering this island and others as seen from the sky. Deep blues and greens characterize his somewhat abstracted vistas, which seem to incorporate the very rush of the plane flying overhead. Looking at Hopkins' work, one is reminded of something Anne Lindbergh wrote in *North to the Orient* about the same area in Maine, viewed from a similar perspective:

> On this swift flight to North Haven in the *Sirius* my mind was so far behind my body that when we flew over Rockland Harbor the familiar landmarks below me had no reality.

While many of the artists active in Maine today try to "make it new," a number of others link up with former generations. A case in point is Frank Mason (b. 1921), whose stormy seascapes carry us back, in an almost uncanny manner, to the work of some of the nineteenth century masters of the bounding main. What one might call a vital revivalist esthetic is being pursued in Mason's work; to a certain extent it also informs the seamless snowscapes of Thomas Crotty (b. 1934) and the classicist landscapes of Thomas Cornell (b. 1937).

Although not quite as different as chalk and cheese, the responses to the Maine coastline of Gina Werfel (b. 1951) and Nancy Wisseman-Widrig (b. 1929) seem poles apart. Werfel, who works on Isleboro, builds up her pigments to match the intractable beauty of rocks and chill waters, while Wisseman-Widrig tends to paint thin, preferring the sparkling aspects of Maine islands and gardens.

There is still the summertime influx of easel-bearing individuals into Maine, but more and more artists are moving north for good, drawn, as in days of yore, by the promise of clean air, room to move and more potential motifs than you can shake a brush at. The number of Maine-born artists is on the rise as well; and the Skowhegan School of Painting and Sculpture, the Haystack Mountain School of Crafts, the University of Maine and the Portland School of Art, among other institutions, turn out important crops of painters each year.

Another formidable change in Maine art is gender-related: where an exhibition of landscape paintings twenty years ago could get away with including only three women artists out of nearly a hundred, such a ratio is no longer possible. Denny Winters, Emily Muir, Brita Holmquist, Dorothy Eisner, Gretna Campbell, Lois Dodd, Sharon Yates, Abby Shahn, Dozier Bell—the roster of women painters who have significantly furthered the art of the landscape over the past forty years or so is a long and impressive one. Earlier eras also yield artistic finds such as Elizabeth B. Robinson (1832–1897), whose *View of North Monmouth, Maine* (c. 1862) evokes a way of life still found in Maine.

In mounting several exhibitions consecrated to pioneer women artists of Maine, the Joan Whitney Payson Gallery of Art at Westbrook College has helped bring to light a number of lesser-known painters—Mabel May Woodward, Augusta Knopf, Sarah Freedman McPherson, et al.—as well as famous painters whose Maine works have not received due attention. In this latter category, two names stand out: Georgia O'Keeffe (1887–1986), who did work at York Beach in the 1920s, and Louise Nevelson (1900–1988), a Russian-born but Rockland-bred sculptor, who also turned out some remarkable landscapes in the early years of her career.

As MAINE approaches the twenty-first century, the choice of landscape subject is changing. Even as many an artist continues to seek out the hidden cove, the secluded stream, the perfect grove of birch trees, others are busy dealing with the monuments of a modern industrial society. The wide-angle views of Maine bridges, dams and large-scale construction sites by Rackstraw Downes (b. 1939) bespeak one who is enamored with, yet taken aback by, the spectacle of man-made superstructures. In a like manner, Yvonne Jacquette (b. 1934) makes an airborne view of the Maine Yankee nuclear power plant appear both romantic and fearsome.

Of course, some subject matter has gone the way of the wind, and history. Clipper ships at anchor in a still harbor used to be a favorite motif for marine painters in this state, but, to my knowledge, no one has expressed a similar affection for the megayachts that clog the waterways of today's Maine.

As the natural resources of the planet dwindle, the landscape of Maine, and the depictions of it, become all the more precious. In the opinions of many, Maine and the world in general are headed for ultimate destruction; for others, solutions are at hand. In the poignant conclusion to *Maine Memories* (1968), Elizabeth Coatsworth, one of the state's greatest writers, offers a prescriptive course of action that I believe would match the sentiments of most Maine painters, past and present:

> And if Americans are to become really at home in America it must be through the devotion of many people to many small, deeply loved places. The field by the sea, the single mountain peak seen from a man's door, the island of trees and farm buildings in the western wheat, must be sung and painted and praised until each takes on the gentleness of the thing long loved, and becomes an unconscious part of us and we of it.

The artists in this book have all, in one way or another, devoted themselves to such "small, deeply loved places." Most of them have gone beyond mere scenery to capture an essence, a quality of light and landscape which belongs to Maine. Even as they heighten our appreciation of a particular view, they also preserve it; and such acts of preservation will be essential to Maine's future—proof of a beauty which knows no bounds.

Carl Little
Mount Desert, 1990

FRANK MASON. Bald Head, Maine, 1984, Oil on canvas, 48 x 60 inches

HE WHO LOOKS ON NATURE WITH A "LOVING EYE,"
cannot move from his dwelling without the salutation of beauty; even in the city the
deep blue sky and the drifting clouds appeal to him. And if to escape its turmoil—if only
to obtain a free horizon, land and water in the play of light and shadow yields delight—
let him be transported to those favored regions, where the features of the earth are
more varied, or yet add the sunset, that wreath of glory daily bound around the world,
and he, indeed, drinks from pleasure's purest cup. The delight such a man experiences
is not merely sensual, or selfish, that passes with the occasion leaving no trace behind;
but in gazing on the pure creations of the Almighty, he feels a calm religious tone
steal through his mind, and when he has turned to mingle with his fellow men,
the chords which have been struck in that sweet communion cease not to vibrate.

THOMAS COLE, *Essay on American Scenery,* 1836

THOMAS COLE, Frenchman's Bay, Mt. Desert Island, Maine, 1845, Oil on wood panel, 13½ x 22⅞ inches

THOMAS COLE, View Across Frenchman's Bay from Mount Desert Island, After A Squall, 1845, Oil on canvas, 38½ x 62 inches

THIS is no sleepy land where lotus grows,
No place of indolence and languid doze
With dulcet winds and warm, seductive seas
To lull and woo you to a soft repose.
No plumage of palm fronds a silken strand.
Spear-head spruce, needle-sharp, secure a land
Whose sea-shocked cliffs neither yield nor appease.
Rock, here, has no plan ever to be sand.

CHARLES E. WADSWORTH, *The Coast of Maine*

UNKNOWN, The Wreck of the Hanover at the Mouth of the Kennebec River, nineteenth century, Oil on canvas, 38¼ x 40¼ inches

THOMAS DOUGHTY, Desert Rock Lighthouse, Mt. Desert, 1847, Oil on canvas, 27 x 41 inches

ALVAN FISHER, Camden Harbor, c. 1850, Oil on canvas, 27 x 36 inches

FREDERIC E. CHURCH, Coast at Mount Desert Island, c. 1850, Oil over graphite on cardboard, 12 x 16 inches

FREDERIC E. CHURCH, Great Basin, Mount Katahdin, Maine, c. 1875-80, Oil over slight traces of graphite on cardboard, 12 x 12 15/16 inches   37

MANY MEN NEED THE WILDERNESS AND THE MOUNTAINS

Katahdin is the best mountain in the wildest wild to be had on this side of the continent.

THEODORE WINTHROP, *Life in the Open Air*, 1856

FREDERIC E. CHURCH, Sunset, 1856, Oil on canvas, 24 x 36 inches

FITZ HUGH LANE, Lumber Schooners at Evening on Penobscot Bay, 1860, Oil on canvas, 24⅛ x 38⅛ inches

CHARLES CODMAN, Entertainment of the Boston Rifle Rangers by the Portland Rifle Club in Portland Harbor, August 12, 1829, 1830
Oil on panel, 24⅜ x 32½ inches

41

JOHN BRADLEY HUDSON, JR., White Head, Cushing Island, Maine, date unknown, Oil on canvas, 38 x 26 inches

THE BACKGROUND OF SEA, THE SEA GULLS SLANTING BY OVERHEAD,
the oxen at work, the boy's voice shouting, the beat of the waves below on the cliffs
and the sound of the bell buoy on the long reef which juts out beyond the end
of the point, all combined to create that sense of man and his surroundings in harmony,
in beauty, which alone can be the base of a real community or civilization.

ELIZABETH COATSWORTH, *Background of Sea,* 1968

WINSLOW HOMER, Maine Cliffs, 1883, Watercolor over charcoal, 13⅜ x 19⅛ inches

WINSLOW HOMER, Prout's neck, Surf on Rocks, 1895, Watercolor over graphite on off-white wove paper, 15⅛ x 21½ inches

WINSLOW HOMER, Early Morning after a Storm at Sea, 1902, Oil on canvas, 30¼ x 50 inches

LOOK AT A HOMER SEASCAPE, THERE IS ORDER IN IT
and grand formation. It produces on your mind the whole vastness of the sea, a vastness
as impressive and as uncontrollable as the sea itself. You are made to feel the force
of the sea, the resistance of the rock; the whole thing is an integrity of nature.

ROBERT HENRI, *The Art Spirit*, 1923

WINSLOW HOMER, The Backrush, c. 1890, Oil on canvas, 29 x 22 inches

WINSLOW HOMER, The Artist's Studio in an Afternoon Fog, 1894, Oil on canvas, 24 x 30 inches

MAURICE PRENDERGAST, The Stony Beach, Ogunquit, 1901
Watercolor on paper, 20⅞ x 13⅞ inches

EDWARD WILLIS REDFIELD, Monhegan Village, date unknown, Oil on canvas, 26 x 32 inches

MAURICE PRENDERGAST, Barn, Brooksville, Maine, c. 1918, Oil on panel, 13⅜ x 10¼ inches

CHILDE HASSAM, Poppies on the Isles of Shoals, 1890, Oil on canvas, 18⅛ x 22⅛ inches

FRANK W. BENSON, Summer, 1909, Oil on canvas, 36⅜ x 44⅜ inches *(opposite)*

THE SEA IS ROSY, AND THE SKY;
the line of land is radiant, the scattered sails glow with the delicious color that touches so
tenderly the bare, bleak rocks. These are lovelier than sky or sea or distant sails, or graceful
gulls' wings reddened with the dawn; nothing takes color so beautifully as the bleached
granite; the shadows are delicate, and the fine, hard outlines are glorified and softened
beneath the fresh first blush of sunrise.

CELIA THAXTER, *Among the Isles of Shoals*, 1873

CHILDE HASSAM, Sunday Morning, Appledore, 1912, Watercolor, 13¾ x 19¾ inches

CHARLES H. WOODBURY, *Phlox #2*, date unknown, Oil on canvas, 29 x 36 inches

MABEL MAY WOODWARD, Seaside, Ogunquit, Maine, c. 1925, Oil on canvas, 16 x 20 inches

ROBERT HENRI, Storm Tide, 1903, Oil on canvas, 26 x 32 inches

N. C. WYETH, Cannibal Shore, 1930, Oil on canvas, 30 x 47½ inches

George Wesley Bellows, The Big Dory, 1913, Oil on canvas, 18 x 22 inches

George Wesley Bellows, Shipyard Society, 1916, Oil on panel, 30 x 38 inches *(opposite)*

FARTHER up the bay the islands still have meadows
And beaches that are sheltered from the rolling ocean swell
And sheep climb up pianos in empty houses on the islands
And the noise they make is harmonious to the private island ear
And the gardening of cropping sheep is beautiful on meadow ledges
While fog pours in the wind from the cold and sunny ocean.

FAIRFIELD PORTER, *Penobscot Bay,* 1985

GEORGE WESLEY BELLOWS, Criehaven, 1917, Oil on canvas, 30 x 44 inches

EDWARD HOPPER, Rocky Projection at the Sea, 1916-19, Oil on composition board, 9 x 12⅞ inches

EDWARD HOPPER, Blackhead, Monhegan, 1916-19, Oil on canvas, 9½ x 13 inches

EDWARD HOPPER, The Dories, Ogunquit, 1914, Oil on canvas, 24 x 29 inches

EDWARD HOPPER, Lighthouse Hill, 1927, Oil on canvas, 28¼ x 39½ inches

NILES SPENCER. The Cove-Ogunquit, 1922, Oil on canvas, 28 x 36 inches

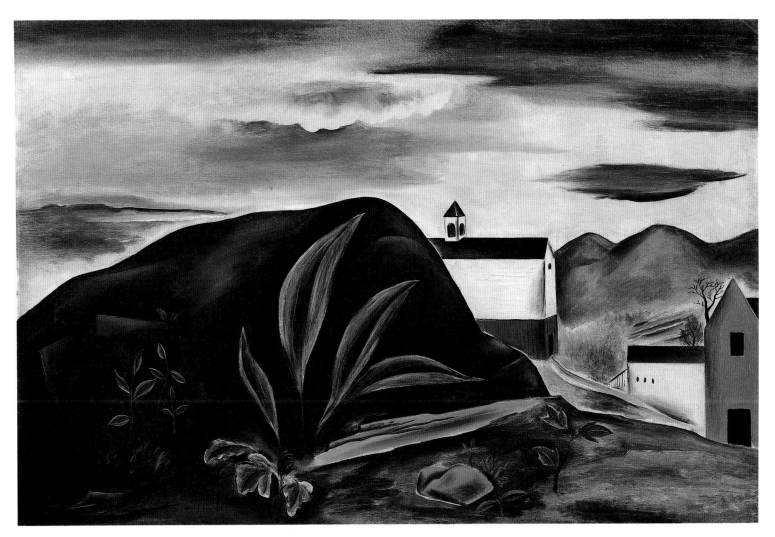

YASUO KUNIYOSHI, Landscape, 1924, Oil on canvas, 20 x 30 inches

I LOVED RUNNING DOWN THE BOARD WALK TO THE OCEAN—
watching the waves come in, spreading over the hard wet beach—the lighthouse steadily
bright far over the waves in the evening when it was almost dark....

GEORGIA O'KEEFFE, in *Georgia O'Keeffe*, 1976

GEORGIA O'KEEFFE, Wave, Night, 1928, Oil on canvas, 30 x 36 inches

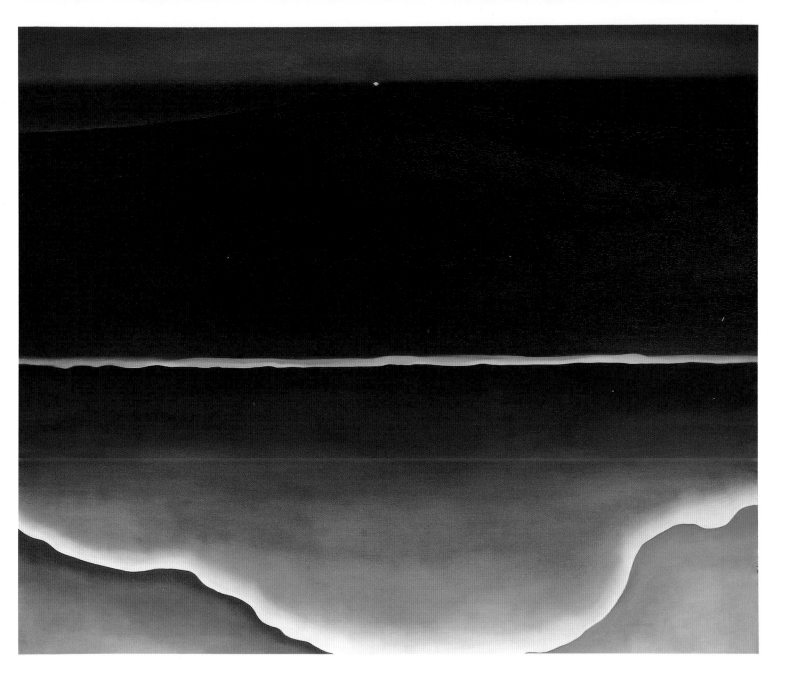

Y<small>ES, SUNDAY IT WAS ALONG ALL THE BEAUTIFUL SHORES</small>
of Maine — netted in green and azure by its thousand islands, all glorious with their
majestic pines, all musical and silvery with the caresses of the sea-waves, that loved to
wander and lose themselves in their numberless shelly coves and tiny beaches
among their cedar shadows.

H<small>ARRIET</small> B<small>EECHER</small> S<small>TOWE</small>, *The Pearl of Orr's Island,* 1862

N. C. W<small>YETH</small>, Island Funeral, 1939, Tempera on panel, 47½ x 55¼ inches

Carl Sprinchorn. Lightning over Millinocket, c. 1925, Oil on canvas, 28 1/8 x 33 1/2 inches

CARL SPRINCHORN. Daisy Fields and Clouds, 1950, Oil on canvas, 21¼ x 29⅛ inches

MARGUERITE ZORACH, Bridge to the Island, 1930, Oil on canvas, 23 x 28 inches

LOUISE NEVELSON, Maine Meadows, Old County Road, c. 1930s, Oil on board, 30¾ x 36¾ inches

MARSDEN HARTLEY, Mount Katahdin, Maine, First Snow, No. 1, c. 1939-40, Oil on board, 22 x 28 inches

While Descending from Mt. Katahdin

I stand in awe of my body, this matter to which I am bound has become so strange to me. I fear not spirits, ghosts, of which I am one, — *that* my body might, — but I fear bodies, I tremble to meet them. What is this Titan that has possession of me? Talk of mysteries! Think of our life in nature, — daily to be shown matter, to come in contact with it, — rocks, trees, wind on our cheeks! the solid earth! the *actual* world! the *common sense!* *Contact! Contact! Who* are we? *where* are we?

HENRY DAVID THOREAU, *The Maine Woods,* 1834

MARSDEN HARTLEY, Crashing Wave, c. 1938, Oil on board, 18 x 24 inches

MARSDEN HARTLEY, Storm Down Pine Point Way, Old Orchard Beach, Maine, c. 1941-43, Oil on masonite, 22 x 28 inches

JOHN MARIN, *Deer Isle Series: Mark Island Lighthouse*, 1928, Watercolor on paper, 16½ x 21¾ inches

WILLIAM ZORACH, Beach at Bay Point, 1946, Watercolor on paper, 15½ x 22½ inches

OLD MISTRESS—MAINE—SHE MAKES YOU TO—LUG—LUG—LUG
—she makes you to—pull—pull—pull—she makes you to—haul—haul—haul
—and when she's thrashed you a plenty—between those thrashings

she's lovely

she smiles

she's beautiful

with an unforgettable loveliness—an unforgettable beauty
—Turns masculine—borders big and mighty—against—the big and mighty Atlantic—

JOHN MARIN, letter to Alfred Stieglitz, Aug. 28, 1932

JOHN MARIN, My Hell Raising Sea, 1941, Oil on canvas, 25 x 30 inches

ANTONIO MATTEI. Snow Storm, Maine Coast, c. 1945, Oil on board, 16¼ x 42 inches

LIVING ON AN ISLAND IS ABOUT THE BEST WAY
there is left to live. It is the nearest we can come to living in Plymouth in 1621. There is
something about living on an island that is like no other thing. Some day I am going to
write a book about it.

ROBERT P. TRISTRAM COFFIN, *Mainstays of Maine*, 1945

NANCY WISSEMANN-WIDRIG, Diderot Island, 1983, Oil on canvas, 40 x 68 inches

THROUGH THIS PIECE OF ROUGH PASTURE RAN A HUGE SHAPE
of stone like the great backbone of an enormous creature. At the end, near the woods,
we could climb up on it and walk along to the highest point; there above the circle of
pointed firs we could look down over all the island, and could see the ocean that circled this
and a hundred other bits of island-ground, the mainland shore and all the far horizons.
It gave a sudden sense of space, for nothing stopped the eye or hedged one in, — that sense
of liberty in space and time which great prospects always give.

SARAH ORNE JEWETT, *Country of the Pointed Firs*, 1896

ROCKWELL KENT, Lone Rock and Sea, 1950, Oil on canvas, 28 x 44 inches

A LITTLE FARTHER ON, WE COME TO ITS SOLITARY GRAVEYARD, —
a square plot of ground, enclosed by white palings, showing a score of graves marked
only with such rough head and foot stones as could be picked up at random.
Not a line or a letter to tell who the occupants are. Others have their memorials, it is true,
but these are the nameless, the forgotten ones. Nowhere do the dead go so quickly.

SAMUEL ADAMS DRAKE, Monhegan on the Sea in *The Pine Tree Coast*, 1896

ROCKWELL KENT, Memorial Day, 1950, Oil on canvas, 34 x 44 inches

If I LIVED IN AN APARTMENT IN NEW YORK CITY,
I wouldn't know a tenth as many people as I know here on this
island in Maine. The sea brings in fresh air. You feel that
you're standing on the border between the human world and
the rest of the universe.

MARGUERITE YOURCENAR, *With Open Eyes*, 1984

ANDREW WYETH, Her Room, 1963, Tempera on masonite, 25½ x 48½ inches

ALEX KATZ. Late July, 1967, Oil on canvas, 72 x 96 inches

BEYOND the darkness of the trees
The sunlight falling free suggests
A landlocked bay. The eye perceives
The light, at least, and there it rests

Until, distracted, I can look
Away. The air moves every leaf.
The branches bend. The landscape stirs.
Imagination, like belief,

Transforms the world. I look again
Down past the shadow. I can see
The bay and all the land beyond.
And I am where I ought to be.

SAMUEL FRENCH MORSE, *A Kind of View,* 1964

FAIRFIELD PORTER, Lobster Pots & Boat House-Afternoon, c. 1970, Oil on canvas, 48¼ x 60 inches

THOMAS CORNELL, Harpswell, 1984, Oil on canvas, 24 x 36 inches

THERE you row with tranquil oars, and the ocean
Shows no scar from the cutting of your placid keel;
Care becomes senseless there; pride and promotion
Remote; you only look; you scarcely feel.

Even adventure, with its vital uses,
Is aimless ardor now; and thrift is waste.

Oh, to be there, under the silent spruces,
Where the wide, quiet evening darkens without haste
Over a sea with death acquainted, yet forever chaste.

EDNA ST. VINCENT MILLAY, excerpt from *Ragged Island*, 1954

FAIRFIELD PORTER. The Dock, 1974-75, Oil on canvas, 21¾ x 37 inches

JAMIE WYETH, Bronze Age, 1967, Oil on canvas, 24 x 36 inches

JAMIE WYETH, Gull Rock, 1970, Oil on canvas, 25 x 40⅛ inches

DURING THE DEPRESSION A MARTHA'S VINEYARD FISHERMAN,
who had learned and practiced his navigation among the shifting sandbars of his home
territory, was driven to accept a job as captain of a yacht bound to the Maine coast.
Three weeks later, from some point east of Frenchman's Bay, he wrote to his wife:
"Marthy, when I die, don't put a stone at the head of my grave; give me a bucket of sand:
I've seen enough rocks to last all eternity."

EDWARD M. HOLMES, from the introduction to *A Part of the Main*, 1973

JAMIE WYETH, Kent House, 1972, Oil on canvas, 30 x 40⅛ inches

NEIL WELLIVER, Burnt Barren, 1981, Oil on canvas, 96 x 96 inches

ALAN BRAY, Ghost on Flanders Hill, 1982, Tempera on wood, 20 x 26 inches

AT night the close cold is still,
the tilt world returns from sun to ice.
Glazed lichen is North, and snowfall

five below. North is where rockface
and hoarfrost are formed with double grace:
love is twice warm in a cold place.

PHILIP BOOTH, *North,* 1986

THOMAS CROTTY, Snow Ledges, 1990, Oil on canvas, 48 x 60 inches

MILTON AVERY, Hills at Rosy Dawn, 1962, Oil on canvas, 36 x 50 inches

KARL SCHRAG, Dawn, Noon & Night, 1990, Oil on canvas, 48 x 60 inches

I<small>F THERE IS ONE WAY ABOVE ANOTHER</small>
of getting so close to nature that one simply is a piece of
nature, following a primeval instinct with perfect
self-forgetfulness and forgetting everything except the dreamy
consciousness of pleasant freedom, it is to take the course of
a shady trout brook. The dark pools and the sunny shallows
beckon one on; the wedge of sky between the trees on either
bank, the speaking, companioning noise of the water, the
amazing importance of what one is doing, and the constant
sense of life and beauty make a strange transformation
of the quick hours.

S<small>ARAH</small> O<small>RNE</small> J<small>EWETT</small>, *Country of the Pointed Firs,* 1896

D<small>AHLOV</small> I<small>PCAR</small>, Rangeley October, 1984, Oil on canvas, 36 x 72 inches

ERIC HOPKINS, Flying Over Harbor Island III, 1986, Oil on canvas, 36 x 48 inches

YVONNE JACQUETTE, Maine Yankee VI, 1983, Oil on canvas, 79 x 70 inches *(opposite)*

WHAT HAPPENS TO ME WHEN I CROSS THE PISCATAQUA
and plunge rapidly into Maine at a cost of seventy-five cents in tolls? I cannot describe it.
I do not ordinarily spy a partridge in a pear tree, or three French hens, but I do
have the sensation of having received a gift from a true love.

E. B. WHITE, *Home-Coming*, 1979

RUSH BROWN, Torsey Pond, 1990, Oil on canvas, 60 x 72 inches

R A C K S T R A W D O W N E S, The Mouth Of The Passagassawaukeag at Belfast, Maine, Seen from the Frozen Foods Plant, 1989,

Oil on canvas (2 panels) 36⅜ x 84¼ inches

Artists' Biographies

MILTON AVERY (1885–1965). Traveled to Maine as early as 1930; spent summer of 1948 at Pemaquid Point; occasional visits later on.

GEORGE WESLEY BELLOWS (1882–1925). Arrived on Monhegan Island July 1911 in the company of Robert Henri and Randall Davey; several prolific summers spent there, with stays in Ogunquit and Camden as well.

FRANK W. BENSON (1862–1951). Summer resident of North Haven Island from 1901 until around 1941.

ALAN BRAY (b. 1946). Born in Waterville, brought up in Monson, now resides in Dover-Foxcroft year-round.

RUSH BROWN (b. 1948). New Canaan, Connecticut native; has worked in Maine since 1963, specializing in inland views: Reedfield, Wales, North Monmouth, etc.

WILLIAM PARTRIDGE BURPEE (1846–1940). Rockland, Maine native; marine painter; worked on Monhegan and in other Maine locales.

FREDERIC E. CHURCH (1826–1900). First trip to Mount Desert Island in 1850; to Katahdin in 1852; later built a camp on Lake Millinocket.

CHARLES CODMAN (1800–1842). Portland-based artist from 1822 on; known for decorative work, Romantic landscapes and picturesque views of Maine sites.

THOMAS COLE (1801–1848). English-born landscape painter; founder of the Hudson River school; came to Maine in 1844; especially taken with Mount Desert Island.

THOMAS CORNELL (b. 1937). Cleveland, Ohio native; first worked in Maine in early 1960s; has focused on Brunswick and neighboring towns: Harpswell, Pennellville, Topsham, etc.; art professor at Bowdoin College.

THOMAS CROTTY (b. 1934). Maine resident since 1959; paints in a number of seaboard towns, including Freeport, Phippsburg and Indian Point in Georgetown. Opened the state's first year-round commercial gallery (Frost Gully) in 1966.

THOMAS DOUGHTY (1793–1856). Connected, through Thomas Cole, to Hudson River school; made sojourns from Boston to Maine; worked around Mount Desert Island in the 1840s.

RACKSTRAW DOWNES (b. 1939). Summers in Morrill; paints landscapes in different parts of the state: Portland, Belfast, Skowhegan, etc.

STEPHEN MORGAN ETNIER (1903–1984). York, Pennsylvania native; first sailed the Maine coast in 1930; went on to paint in numerous locations, living a large part of his life in the state.

ALVAN FISHER (1792–1863). Boston-based artist; traveled widely in New England; worked in Camden and around Mount Desert Island, among other areas of Maine.

MARSDEN HARTLEY (1877–1943). American modernist; Lewiston-born, left Maine at a young age but returned many times, most critically in late 1930s and early 1940s; worked in Ogunquit, Georgetown, Old Orchard Beach, Corea, etc., and at the base of Mt. Katahdin.

CHILDE HASSAM (1859–1935). Native of Dorchester, Massachusetts; visited Isles of Shoals in early 1880s; painted there during summers well into the next century, primarily on Appledore.

ROBERT HENRI (1865–1929). Ashcan school artist; went to Monhegan in 1903, first of many visits; also painted in and around Boothbay Harbor; author of *The Art Spirit* (1923).

WINSLOW HOMER (1836–1910). Boston-born with Maine roots; settled for good at Prout's Neck in 1884, having first visited the area in 1875.

ERIC HOPKINS (b. 1951). Bangor, Maine native; full-time resident of North Haven Island for a number of years now; glass artist and aerial landscape painter.

EDWARD HOPPER (1882–1967). Initial forays to Maine in mid-1910s to Ogunquit and Monhegan; later did views of Cape Elizabeth, Rockland and Portland.

JOHN BRADLEY HUDSON, JR. (1832–1903). Portland-born landscape and genre painter; active in his native city, Androscoggin County and elsewhere.

DAHLOV IPCAR (b. 1917). Year-round resident of Georgetown Island since 1937; *animalier*, children's book illustrator and landscape painter.

YVONNE JACQUETTE (b. 1934). Arrived in Maine in 1963; stayed in Lincolnville, then nearby Searsmont; also works in and around Belfast and Skowhegan, frequently from the air.

ALEX KATZ (b. 1927). First came to Maine in 1949 to attend Skowhegan School; has summered in Lincolnville since 1954 with studio on Coleman Pond.

ROCKWELL KENT (1882–1971). Invited to Monhegan Island by Robert Henri in 1905; spent next five or so years there; returned to island in late 1940s for a number of summers.

WILLIAM KIENBUSCH (1914–1980). First painted in Maine in 1934–35, in Kennebunkport; worked in Stonington and Trevett; made his way downeast to Great Cranberry Island, where he had his studio from 1962 on.

LEON KROLL (1884–1974). Met Homer at Prout's Neck in 1907; later painted on Monhegan, as well as at Ogunquit, Camden and Deer Isle.

YASUO KUNIYOSHI (1893–1953). Japanese-born; studied with Hamilton Easter Field at Ogunquit in 1918; stayed during summers through 1924.

FITZ HUGH LANE (1804–1865). One of the foremost of the Luminist painters; sailed the Maine coast in mid-1800s to Penobscot Bay, Mount Desert Island and elsewhere.

JOHN MARIN (1870–1953). Made his first claim on the state in 1914 at West Point; significant painting periods at Small Point, Stonington, Tunk Mountain and Cape Split.

FRANK MASON (b. 1921). Arrived in Maine in 1949, painting at Cape Small, near Bath; summers at Bald Head for many years. Professor of art at Art Students League.

ANTONIO MATTEI (1900–1956). Paterson, New Jersey native and New York-based artist; came to Ogunquit in the early 1920s; later stayed year-round.

LOUISE NEVELSON (1900–1988). Born in Russia; moved to Maine in 1905; executed landscapes in the Rockland area in the 1930s before turning to wooden assemblages.

GEORGIA O'KEEFFE (1887–1986). American modernist; made initial trip to York Beach in spring of 1920; worked there on and off until 1928, with a focus on coastal motifs.

FAIRFIELD PORTER (1907–1975). Longtime summer resident of Great Spruce Head Island in Penobscot Bay; also well-known art critic.

MAURICE PRENDERGAST (1861–1924). Directed his Post-Impressionistic style of painting to Maine coast subjects around the turn of the century; worked in Brooksville, Ogunquit and Old Orchard.

EDWARD WILLIS REDFIELD (1869–1965). Pennsylvania impressionist; visited Monhegan with Henri in 1903; summered in Boothbay Harbor.

ELIZABETH B. ROBINSON (1832–1897). Little is known of the life of this painter save that she studied at Litchfield Academy and worked in a naive style.

KARL SCHRAG (b. 1912). German-born, emigrated to the U.S. in 1938; first came to Maine in 1940s; has worked, summers, on Chebeague Island, Friendship, Vinalhaven and, currently, Deer Isle.

NILES SPENCER (1833–1952). Arrived in Ogunquit in 1914 to study with Charles Woodbury; stayed year-round, 1919–22.

CARL SPRINCHORN (1887–1971). Native of Broby, Sweden; traveled to U.S. in 1903; first visited Maine in 1907; worked in and around Swedish colony of Monson in 1917–22, at Shin Pond in 1930s and 40s.

REUBEN TAM (b. 1916). Born in Hawaii; painted on Monhegan from 1948 to 1980, after which he returned to native island of Kauai; poet as well as painter.

NEIL WELLIVER (b. 1929). Year-round resident of Lincolnville; has worked in Maine since early 1960s.

GINA WERFEL (b. 1951). Has taught art at Colby College in Waterville since 1980; paints on Islesboro and in rural Maine (East Vassalboro, etc.)

NANCY WISSEMAN-WIDRIG (b. 1929). Long Island-based artist; has painted summers in Cushing since 1968.

CHARLES H. WOODBURY (1864–1940). Boston art teacher; arrived in Ogunquit in 1888, built studio there in 1896, opened school of art in 1898 (which ran till 1917, then from 1924 to 1940).

MABEL MAY WOODWARD (1877–1945). Resided Providence, Rhode Island; summered in Ogunquit, painting impressionist-inspired seacoast views.

ANDREW WYETH (b. 1917). Realist painter; first came to Maine in his youth; divides time between Chadds Ford, Pennsylvania, and Cushing, Maine; works primarily in tempera and watercolor.

JAMIE WYETH (b. 1946). Has passed summers and falls painting on Monhegan since the mid-1960s; has excelled as landscape painter and portraitist.

N. C. WYETH (1882–1945). Famous illustrator; from 1920–1945 traveled to Port Clyde and later Cushing to paint in oils.

MARGUERITE ZORACH (1887–1968). California native; spent first summer in Maine at Stonington with husband William in 1919; settled in the state in 1923; besides landscapes, also made remarkable embroidered tapestries.

WILLIAM ZORACH (1887–1966). Born in Lithuania; came to America at age four; moved to Maine for good in 1923; known for his sculpture and landscape paintings.

MUSEUM OF ART
Olin Arts Center
Bates College
Lewiston, Maine 04240
Tel. 207-786-6158

Collection: the Museum of Art specializes in 19th and 20th century American and European prints, drawings, and photographs. It also has small holdings in 20th century American paintings. Signficant to the collection is the Marsden Hartley Memorial Collection consisting of 99 drawings, three oil paintings, and memorabilia from the artist's estate. In addition to Hartley, a native of Lewiston, Maine, other artists who lived and worked in Maine are well-represented, including D. D. Coombs, William and Marguerite Zorach, Waldo Pierce, Carl Sprinchorn, and William Thon. The Museum is located in a newly constructed, contemporary-designed building. Its galleries display loaned and permanent collection exhibitions that feature traditional and contemporary art.

Hours: Tues.-Sat., 10:00-5:00; Sun., 1:00-5:00. The Museum is also open during evening concerts at the Olin Arts Center. Closed Mondays and major holidays.
Free and open to the public.

THE WILLIAM A. FARNSWORTH LIBRARY & ART MUSEUM
19 Elm Street, Rockland, Maine 04841
Tel. 207-596-6457

Collection: covering over 200 years of American art, with an emphasis on the art of Maine. Works in all media are represented with particular strengths in American portraiture, American watercolors, 19th and 20th century American landscapes, and American Impressionism. Among the approximately 5000 objects in the collection are important works by Fitz Hugh Lane, George Bellows, Willard Metcalf, Frank Benson, Winslow Homer, John Marin, and Louise Nevelson. Of special note is the Museum's large collection of works by N. C., Andrew and James Wyeth. The Museum also maintains and interprets the Farnsworth Homestead, the Victorian home of the Farnsworth family. The art reference library is open to the public, with research assistance available by appointment.

Hours & Admission: June 1–Sept. 30, Mon.-Sat. 10:00-5:00, Sun. 1:00-5:00; Oct. 1–May 31, Tues.-Sat. 10:00-5:00, Sun. 1:00-5:00. Adults $3.00; Senior Citizens and Students $2; children under 12 admitted free. Closed all major holidays.

THE BOWDOIN COLLEGE MUSEUM OF ART
Walker Art Building
Brunswick, Maine 04011
Tel. 207-725-3275

Collection: the building is an important Charles Follin McKim design, opened to the public in 1894, and collections represent the art of Assyria, Greece and Rome, Asia, Africa, Europe and America; media include painting, sculpture and the decorative arts, prints, drawings, watercolors and photographs; three special collections are the James Bowdoin III collection of European old master drawings, the Molinari medals and plaquettes, and the Winslow Homer collection which includes the artist's correspondence and personal effects. The American and Maine collections are particularly strong: famous portraits include works by Smibert, Feke, Blackburn, Stuart, the Peales, Sully, Sargent, Eakins, etc. There are four important murals in the entry hall by Kenyon Cox, John La Farge, Abbott H. Thayer and Elihu Vedder. Views of Maine include those by Winslow Homer, Rockwell Kent, Marsden Hartley, and Andrew Wyeth. Also worthy of mention is an outstanding group of 19 John Sloan paintings and much of his graphic art. Contemporary art includes a complete subscription to prints of the Vinalhaven Press.

Hours: Tues.-Sat. 10:00-5:00; Sun. 2:00-5:00. Guided tours are available mid-June–August: Tues. and Thurs. at 2:00; Wed. and Fri. at 12:30. Closed Mondays and major holidays. Free admission.

THE JOAN WHITNEY PAYSON GALLERY OF ART
Westbrook College
716 Stevens Ave., Portland, Maine 04103
Tel. 207-797-9546

The Payson Gallery is a small college museum whose core collection is from that of Joan Whitney Payson. The building is a 1977 gift of John W. Payson and Nancy Lawler Payson (WC '60) and many of the works in the Payson Collection are promised gifts. Artists include Chagall, Daumier, Degas, Gauguin, Ingres, Monet, Prendergast, Renoir, Rousseau, and Whistler. Other works given or on long-term loan are by Cassatt, Hofmann, and Utrillo. From fall through spring, a schedule of changing exhibitions features artists from Maine as well as such diverse shows as computer art by Laurence Gartel, the slaughterhouses of Sue Coe, and photographs by Minor White. Cited for being "in the fastest cultural stream in the state," the Payson Gallery is also known in Maine as "the little jewel."

Hours: Tues., Wed., Fri. 10:00-4:00; Thurs. 10:00-9:00; Sat. & Sun. 1:00-5:00. Closed on Mondays and major holidays. Free admission.

COLBY COLLEGE MUSEUM OF ART
Colby College
Waterville, Maine 04901
Tel. 207-872-3228

Collection: focus on American painting from the early 18th century through the present including works by Badger, Smibert, Copley, Earl, Charles Willson Peale, Stuart, Johnson, Homer, Hassam, Chase, Robinson, Bellows, Kent, Kuhn, Guston, Nevelson, Katz, Welliver, and Indiana. Special collections include: the John Marin Collection of 25 works by the artist; the Jetté American Heritage Collection of 76 works by primitive artists; the Helen Warren and Willard Howe Cummings Collection of 19th century American art; and the Jetté American Impressionist Collection of 96 watercolors and paintings. Other collections include an English and European collection with works by Romney, Hopner, Richard Wilson, Horace Vernet, Corot, Utrillo, Dughet, Giordano; decorative arts including the Bernat Collection of Oriental Ceramics with pieces dating from 2500 B.C. to the 19th century; and European and American prints and drawings. Selections from the permanent collection are shown on a rotating basis along with temporary loan exhibitions.

Hours: Mon.-Sat. 10:00-12:00, 1:00–4:30; Sun. 2:00-4:30. Closed major holidays. Free admission.

THE MUSEUM OF ART OF OGUNQUIT
181 Shore Road, P.O. Box 815
Ogunquit, Maine 03907
Tel. 207-646-4909

Called "the most beautiful small museum in the world," the MOAO is located on the rocky coast of Maine approximately 1½ hours from Boston. Its extensive Permanent Collection of 20th century American art includes paintings, drawings, prints, and sculpture by artists such as Peggy Bacon, Romare Bearden, Isabel Bishop, Charles Burchfield, Charles Demuth, John Flannagan, Morris Graves, Marsden Hartley, Rockwell Kent, Walt Kuhn, Yasuo Kuniyoshi, Gaston Lachaise, Jack Levine, George Luks, John Marin, Reginald Marsh, Jules Pascin, Mark Tobey, and Marguerite and William Zorach. In addition to exhibiting its permanent collection, the MOAO features annual summer exhibitions of 20th century American art.

Hours: July 1–Sept. 15, Mon.-Sat. 10:30-5:00, Sun. 1:00-5:00. Closed major holidays. Free admission.

PORTLAND MUSEUM OF ART
Seven Congress Square
Portland, Maine 04101
Tel. 207-775-6148

Located in the heart of downtown Portland, the Portland Museum of Art celebrates the heritage of the State of Maine through its collection and its active exhibition program which expands upon its regional focus. The Museum consists of three architecturally significant buildings: the Charles Shipman Payson Building, designed by the firm of I. M. Pei & Partners, the Federal Period McLellan House, and the Sweat Memorial, a *beaux arts* structure. Founded in 1883, the Museum collection of 12,000 objects includes 18th, 19th, and 20th century painting, sculpture, works on paper, and decorative arts from the United States, Europe, and the Orient. Included in the collection are 17 paintings by Winslow Homer. International traveling exhibitions. Handicapped access. Museum Shop.

Hours & Admission: Tues.-Sat. 10:00-5:00, Thur. 10:00-9:00, Sun. 12:00-5:00. Adults $3.50; Senior Citizens and Students (I.D.) $2.50; Children under 18 $1.00; Group rate $3.00. Free admission Thursdays 5:00-9:00 made possible by UNUM Charitable Foundation. Closed Mondays and major holidays.

Credits

Artist Unknown
*The Wreck of the Hanover at the Mouth
of the Kennebec River*, nineteenth century
Oil on canvas, 38¼ x 40¼ in.
Maine Maritime Museum, Bath, ME
Courtesy Private collection
32

Avery, Milton
Hills at Rosy Dawn, 1962
Oil on canvas, 36 x 50 in.
Collection of Milton & Sally Avery Arts Foundation
Courtesy of Grace Borgenicht Gallery, NY
110

Bellows, George Wesley
Criehaven, 1917
Oil on canvas, 30 x 44 in.
The William Benton Museum of Art
The University of Connecticut
Louise Crombie Beach Memorial Collection
65

Bellows, George Wesley
Romance of Autumn, 1916
Oil on canvas, 32½ x 40 in.
William A. Farnsworth Library and Art Museum
Frontispiece

Bellows, George Wesley
Shipyard Society, 1916
Oil on panel, 30 x 38 in.
Virginia Museum of Fine Arts, Richmond
The Adolph D. & Wilkins C. Williams Fund
63

Bellows, George Wesley
The Big Dory, 1913
Oil on canvas, 18 x 22 in.
New Britain Museum of American Art
Harriet Russell Stanley Fund
62

Benson, Frank W.
Summer, 1909
Oil on canvas, 36⅜ x 44⅜ in.
Museum of Art, Rhode Island School of Design
Bequest of Isaac C. Bates
55

Bray, Alan
Ghost on Flanders Hill, 1982
Tempera on wood, 20 x 26 in.
Collection of the Maine Savings Bank
Photo by Stretch Tuemmier
107

Brown, Rush
Torsey Pond, 1990
Oil on canvas, 60 x 72 in.
Courtesy of Hobe Sound Galleries North
117

Burpee, William Partridge
Misty Morning, Blackhead, c. 1920
Oil on canvas, 6¾ x 12⅛ in.
Courtesy of Childs Gallery, Boston & New York
15

Church, Frederic E.
Coast at Mount Desert Island, c. 1850
Oil over graphite on cardboard, 12 x 16 in.
Courtesy of the Cooper-Hewitt Museum,
Smithsonian Institution / Art Resource, NY
Gift of Louis P. Church, 1917-4-645
Photo by Ken Pelka
36

Church, Frederic E.
Great Basin, Mount Katahdin, Maine, c. 1875-80
Oil over slight traces of graphite on cardboard
12 x 12 15/16 in.
Courtesy of the Cooper-Hewitt Museum,
Smithsonian Institution / Art Resource, NY
Gift of Louis P. Church, 1917-4-632
Photo by Ken Pelka
37

Church, Frederic E.
Sunset, 1856
Oil on canvas, 24 x 36 in.
Proctor Collection, Munson-Williams-Proctor
Institute Museum of Art, Utica, NY
Photo by G. R. Farley
39

Codman, Charles
*Entertainment of the Boston Rifle Rangers
by the Portland Rifle Club in Portland Harbor,
August 12, 1829*, 1830
Oil on panel, 24⅜ x 32½ in.
The Brooklyn Museum
Dick S. Ramsay Fund
41

Cole, Thomas
Frenchman's Bay, Mt. Desert Island, Maine, 1845
Oil on wood panel, 13½ x 22⅞ in.
Albany Institute of History & Art
29

Cole, Thomas
*View Across Frenchman's Bay from Mount
Desert Island, After A Squall*, 1845
Oil on canvas, 38½ x 62 in.
Cincinnati Art Museum
Gift of Alice Scarborough
Photo by Joseph Levy
30-31

Cornell, Thomas
Harpswell, 1984
Oil on canvas, 24 x 36 in.
Bowdoin College Museum of Art, Brunswick, ME
99

Crotty, Thomas
Snow Ledges, 1990
Oil on canvas, 48 x 60 in.
Photo courtesy of Frost Gully Gallery
108

Doughty, Thomas
Desert Rock Lighthouse, Mt. Desert, 1847
Oil on canvas, 27 x 41 in.
The Newark Museum
Gift of Mrs. Jennie E. Mead, 1939
Photo by Armen
34

Downes, Rackstraw
*The Mouth Of The Passagassawaukeag at Belfast,
Maine, Seen from the Frozen Foods Plant*, 1989
Oil on canvas (2 panels), 36⅜ x 84¼ in.
Courtesy of Hirschl & Adler Modern, New York
Photo by Zindman / Fremont
118-119

Etnier, Stephen Morgan
Mid-Channel Bell, 1954
Oil on canvas, 11 x 24 in.
William A. Farnsworth Library and Art Museum
Gift of Mr. Gifford A. Cochran, 1965
13

Fisher, Alvan
Camden Harbor, c. 1850
Oil on canvas, 27 x 36 in.
William A. Farnsworth Library and Art Museum
Gift of Mr. & Mrs. Philip Hofer, 1966
35

Hartley, Marsden
Birds of the Bagaduce, 1939
Oil on canvas, 28 x 22 in.
The Butler Institute of American Art
19

Hartley, Marsden
Crashing Wave, c. 1938
Oil on board, 18 x 24 in.
Courtesy of Salander-O'Reilly
Galleries, Inc., NY & CA.
82

Hartley, Marsden
Mount Katahdin, Maine,
First Snow, No. 1, c. 1939-40
Oil on board, 22 x 28 in.
Courtesy of Salander-O'Reilly
Galleries, Inc., NY & CA
80

Hartley, Marsden
Storm Down Pine Point Way, Old
Orchard Beach, Maine, c. 1941-43
Oil on masonite, 22 x 28 in.
The Regis Collection
83

Hartley, Marsden
Sundown Kezar Lake, 1910
Oil on panel, 5¼ x 9⅜ in.
Bates Collection, Museum of Art, Olin Arts Center
Marsden Hartley Memorial Collection
Photo by Melville McLean
128

Hassam, Childe
August Afternoon — Appledore, 1900
Oil on canvas, 22¼ x 18 in.
Private collection, Texas
Photo by Taggart & Jorgensen Gallery
18

Hassam, Childe
Poppies on the Isles of Shoals, 1890
Oil on canvas, 18⅛ x 22⅛ in.
The Brooklyn Museum
Gift of Mary Pratt Barringer & Richard Pratt, Jr.
in memory of Richardson & Laura Pratt
54

Hassam, Childe
Sunday Morning, Appledore, 1912
Watercolor, 13¾ x 19¾ in.
The Brooklyn Museum
Museum Collection Fund, 1924
56

Henri, Robert
Storm Tide, 1903
Oil on canvas, 26 x 32 in.
Whitney Museum of American Art
Purchase 31.242
Photo by Robert E. Mates Studio, NJ
60

Homer, Winslow
The Backrush, c. 1890
Oil on canvas, 29 x 22 in.
The Joan Whitney Payson Collection
The Joan Whitney Payson Gallery of Art
Westbrook College, Portland, ME
Gift of Joan Whitney Payson
Photo by Benjamin Magro
48

Homer, Winslow
Early Morning after a Storm at Sea, 1902
Oil on canvas, 30¼ x 50 in.
The Cleveland Museum of Art
Gift of J. H. Wade
46

Homer, Winslow
Maine Cliffs, 1883
Watercolor over charcoal, 13⅜ x 19⅛ in.
The Brooklyn Museum
Bequest of Sidney B. Curtis
in memory of S. W. Curtis
44

Homer, Winslow
Prout's Neck, Surf on Rocks, 1895
Watercolor over graphite on off-white
wove paper, 15⅛ x 21½ in.
Worcester Art Museum, Worcester, MA
45

Homer, Winslow
The Artist's Studio in an Afternoon Fog, 1894
Oil on canvas, 24 x 30 in.
Memorial Art Gallery of the University
of Rochester, R. T. Miller Fund
49

Hopkins, Eric
Flying Over Harbor Island III, 1986
Oil on canvas, 36 x 48 in.
Collection of Mr. & Mrs. Stephen Weston
Courtesy of the artist
Photo by William Thuss
115

Hopper, Edward
Blackhead, Monhegan, 1916-19
Oil on canvas, 9½ x 13 in.
Whitney Museum of American Art
Josephine N. Hopper Bequest, 70.1317
Photo by Robert E. Mates, NJ
67

Hopper, Edward
Lighthouse Hill, 1927
Oil on canvas, 28¼ x 39½ in.
Dallas Museum of Art
Gift of Mr. & Mrs. Maurice Purnell
Photo by Geoffrey Clements, NY
69

Hopper, Edward
Rocky Projection at the Sea, 1916-19
Oil on composition board, 9 x 12⅞ in.
Whitney Museum of American Art
Joseph N. Hopper Bequest, 70.1310
Photo by Geoffrey Clements, NY
66

Hopper, Edward
The Dories, Ogunquit, 1914
Oil on canvas, 24 x 29 in.
Whitney Museum of American Art
Joseph N. Hopper Bequest, 70.1196
Photo by Geoffrey Clements, NY
68

Hudson, Jr., John Bradley
White Head, Cushing Island, Maine, date unknown
Oil on canvas, 38 x 26 in.
Portland Museum of Art
Purchase with gifts from Vassar College alumnae
in memory of Janet Hickey Drummond, 1979
42

Ipcar, Dahlov
Rangeley October, 1984
Oil on canvas, 36 x 72 in.
Collection of Mr. & Mrs. C. David O'Brien
Courtesy of Frost Gully Gallery
Photo by Jay York
112-113

Jacquette, Yvonne
Maine Yankee VI, 1983
Oil on canvas, 79 x 70 in.
Private collection
Courtesy of Brooke Alexander Gallery, New York
114

Katz, Alex
Late July, 1967
Oil on canvas, 72 x 96 in.
Collection of the artist
Courtesy of the Marlborough Gallery, Inc.
96

Kent, Rockwell
Lone Rock and Sea, 1950
Oil on canvas, 28 x 44 in.
William A. Farnsworth Library and Art Museum
91

Kent, Rockwell
Memorial Day, 1950
Oil on canvas, 34 x 44 in.
Courtesy of the Rockwell Kent Legacies and
The Suny Plattsburgh Art Museum
92

Kent, Rockwell
Toilers of the Sea, 1907
Oil on canvas, 38 x 44 in.
New Britain Museum of American Art
Charles F. Smith Fund
10

Kienbusch, William
Across Penobscot Bay, 1955
Gouache on paper, 27 x 40½ in.
The Museum of Fine Arts, Houston
Museum purchase
9

Kroll, Leon
Monhegan Landscape, 1913
Oil on canvas, 8¾ x 10¾ in.
Bowdoin College Museum of Art, Brunswick, ME
Title page

Kuniyoshi, Yasuo
Landscape, 1924
Oil on canvas, 20 x 30 in.
Whitney Museum of American Art, 31.271
Photo by Sheldon C. Collins, NY
71

Lane, Fitz Hugh
*Lumber Schooners at Evening on
Penobscot Bay*, 1860
Oil on canvas, 24⅛ x 38⅛ in.
National Gallery of Art, Washington
Andrew W. Mellon Fund
Gift of Mr. & Mrs. Francis W. Hatch, Sr.
40

Marin, John
Deer Isle Series: Mark Island Lighthouse, 1928
Watercolor on paper, 16½ x 21¾ in.
Portland Museum of Art
Gift of Mr. & Mrs. John Marin, Jr., 1982
84

Marin, John
My Hell Raising Sea, 1941
Oil on canvas, 25 x 30 in.
Collection of Barney A. Ebsworth
86

Mason, Frank
Bald Head, Maine, 1984
Oil on canvas, 48 x 60 in.
Collection of the artist
Photo by Tony Mysak
27

Mattei, Antonio
Snow Storm, Maine Coast, c. 1945
Oil on board, 16¼ x 42 in.
The Museum of Art of Ogunquit
88

Nevelson, Louise
Maine Meadows Old County Road, c. 1930s
Oil on board, 30¾ x 36¾ in.
William A. Farnsworth Library and Art Museum
79

O'Keeffe, Georgia
Wave, Night, 1928
Oil on canvas, 30 x 36 in.
Addison Gallery of American Art
Phillips Academy, Andover, MA
Gift of Charles L. Stillman
73

Porter, Fairfield
The Dock, 1974-75
Oil on canvas, 21¾ x 37 in.
William A. Farnsworth Library and Art Museum
100-101

Porter, Fairfield
Lobster Pots & Boat House—Afternoon, c. 1970
Oil on canvas, 48¼ x 60 in.
Collection of B. E. A. Associates
Courtesy of Hirschl & Adler Modern, NY
98

Prendergast, Maurice
The Stony Beach, Ogunquit, 1901
Watercolor on paper, 20⅞ x 13⅞ in.
Collection of Arthur G. Altschul
50, 51

Prendergast, Maurice
Barn, Brooksville, Maine, c. 1918
Oil on panel, 13⅜ x 10¼ in.
Colby College Museum of Art
53

Redfield, Edward Willis
Monhegan Village, date unknown
Oil on canvas, 26 x 32 in.
Private collection, California
Photo by Taggart & Jorgensen Gallery
52

Robinson, Elizabeth B.
View of North Monmouth, Maine, c. 1862
Pastel on paper, 15½ x 21½ in.
Bowdoin College Museum of Art, Brunswick, ME
6

Schrag, Karl
Dawn, Noon & Night, 1990
Oil on canvas, 48 x 60 in.
Courtesy of Kraushaar Galleries
111

Spencer, Niles
The Cove—Ogunquit, 1922
Oil on canvas, 28 x 36 in.
The Newark Museum
Purchase 1926
Photo by Witt
70

Sprinchorn, Carl
Daisy Fields and Clouds, 1950
Oil on canvas, 21¼ x 29⅛ in.
Courtesy of Sordoni Art Gallery
Wilkes University
77

Sprinchorn, Carl
Lightning over Millinocket, c. 1925
Oil on canvas, 28⅛ x 33½ in.
Portland Museum of Art
76

Tam, Reuben
Ocean Morning, 1957
Oil on canvas, 36 x 45 in.
Hirshhorn Museum and Sculpture Garden
Smithsonian Institution
Gift of Joseph H. Hirshhorn, 1966
Photo by Lee Stalsworth
20

Welliver, Neil
Burnt Barren, 1981
Oil on canvas, 96 x 96 in.
Rahr-West Art Museum
106

Welliver, Neil
Drowned Cedars, 1977
Oil on canvas, 96 x 120 in.
Collection of Marlborough Gallery, NY
17

Werfel, Gina
Rocks at High Tide, 1988
Oil on linen, 28 x 36 in.
Private collection
Courtesy of Prince Street Gallery, NY
7

Wissemann-Widrig, Nancy
Diderot Island, 1983
Oil on canvas, 40 x 68 in.
Private collection
89

Woodbury, Charles H.
Phlox #2, date unknown
Oil on canvas, 29 x 36 in.
Courtesy of Vose Galleries, Boston
Photo courtesy of Clive Russ
58

Woodward, Mabel May
Seaside, Ogunquit, Maine, c. 1925
Oil on canvas, 16 x 20 in.
The William Benton Museum of Art
The University of Connecticut
Gift of Edward L. Shein
59

Wyeth, Andrew
Her Room, 1963
Tempera on masonite, 25½ x 48½ in.
William A. Farnsworth Library and Art Museum
94-95

Wyeth, Andrew
Night Hauling, 1944
Tempera on canvas, 23 x 37¼ in.
Bowdoin College Museum of Art, Brunswick, ME
23

Wyeth, Jamie
Bronze Age, 1967
Oil on canvas, 24 x 36 in.
William A. Farnsworth Library and Art Museum
102

Wyeth, Jamie
Excursion Boats, 1982
Mixed media on paper, 25¼ x 36⅝ in.
Private collection
Courtesy of Coe Kerr Gallery
24

Wyeth, Jamie
Gull Rock, 1970
Oil on canvas, 25 x 40⅛ in.
Private collection
Courtesy of Coe Kerr Gallery
103

Wyeth, Jamie
Kent House, 1972
Oil on canvas, 30 x 40⅛ in.
Private collection
Courtesy of Coe Kerr Gallery
104

Wyeth, N. C.
Cannibal Shore, 1930
Oil on canvas, 30 x 47½ in.
William A. Farnsworth Library and Art Museum
61

Wyeth, N. C.
Portrait of a Young Artist, [Andrew Wyeth] c. 1930
Oil on canvas, 32 x 40 in.
William A. Farnsworth Library and Art Museum
Half-title page

Wyeth, N. C.
Island Funeral, 1939
Tempera on panel, 47½ x 55¼ in.
The Hotel Dupont Collection
Photo courtesy of Brandywine River Museum
74

Zorach, Marguerite
Bridge to the Island, 1930
Oil on canvas, 23 x 28 in.
Collection of Timothy, Peter, & Jonathan Zorach
Photo by Tannery Hill, Thopsham, ME
78

Zorach, William
Beach at Bay Point, 1946
Watercolor on paper, 15½ x 22½ in.
Portland Museum of Art
Gift of the Zorach family: Tessim Zorach
& Dahlov Zorach Ipcar, 1971
85

MARSDEN HARTLEY, Sundown Kezar Lake, 1910, Oil on panel, 5¼ x 9⅜ inches